MW01593816

Super Cheap Dubai Travel Guide 2019

Contents

Our Mission

Travel guides show you pricey accommodation and restaurants because they make money OFF OF YOU. Travel bloggers and influencers often do the same. Super Cheap Guides help you use the system against itself to experience unforgettable trips that will blow your mind, not your budget.

We believe that travel can and is best enjoyed on a budget. We work to dispel myths, save you tons of money and help you find experiences that will flash before your eyes when you come to take your last breath on this beautiful earth.

Perhaps the biggest money saving trick you can employ is to know what you want to spend on and what you don't. This guide focuses on the cheap or free, but we do include the unique things to experience in our worth the fee section. There is little use travelling somewhere and not experiencing all it has to offer. Where possible we've included cheap workarounds.

We are the first travel guide company to include Airbnb's in our recommendations, if you think any of these need updating you can email me at philgtang@gmail.com

Who this book is for and why budget travel can be enjoyed by anyone?

Friends and family constantly ask me 'How can you afford to travel?' my response 'I have a unique skill and passion for finding bargains'. This doesn't mean I do any less or sleep in dirty hostels. Someone who spends A LOT on travel hasn't planned or wants to spend their money. I have formulated a system - which I hope to pass on to you in my travel guides - to juice everything from my travel adventures, while spending the least possible money.

There is a difference between being cheap and frugal - I like to spend money on beautiful experiences, but 18 years of travel has taught me I could have a 20 cent experience that will stir my soul more than a $100 dollar one. Of course, there are times when the reverse is true, my point is, spending money on travel is the best investment you can make but it doesn't have to be at levels set by hotels and attractions with massive ad spends and influencers who are paid small fortunes to get you to buy into something that you could have for a fraction of the cost.

Talking of 'the gram'. I've never used it, and probably never will though I have many friends who text me when they find good discounts on it or Twitter/Facebook, I love travelling so much because it forces me to be present minded. I like to have the cold hard budget busting facts to hand (which is why I've included so many one page charts), but otherwise I want to shape my own experience - and I'm sure you do to.

I have designed these travel guides to give you a unique planning tool to experience a soul-stirring trip without spending the ascribed tourist budget.

When it comes to FUN budget travel, it's all about what you know. You can have all the feels without most of the bills. A hour spent planning can save you hundreds on the same maybe even thousands on the same experiences. Travel Addict Guides have done the planning for you, so you can focus on what matters: immersing yourself in the sights, sounds and smells, meeting awesome people and most importantly, being relaxed and happy. My sincere hope is that my tips will bring you great joy at a fraction of the price most people recommend.

So, grab a cup of tea, put your feet up and relax; you're about to enter the world of enjoying Dubai on the cheap. Oh and never forget a biscuit with the tea. You need energy to plan a trip of a lifetime on a budget.

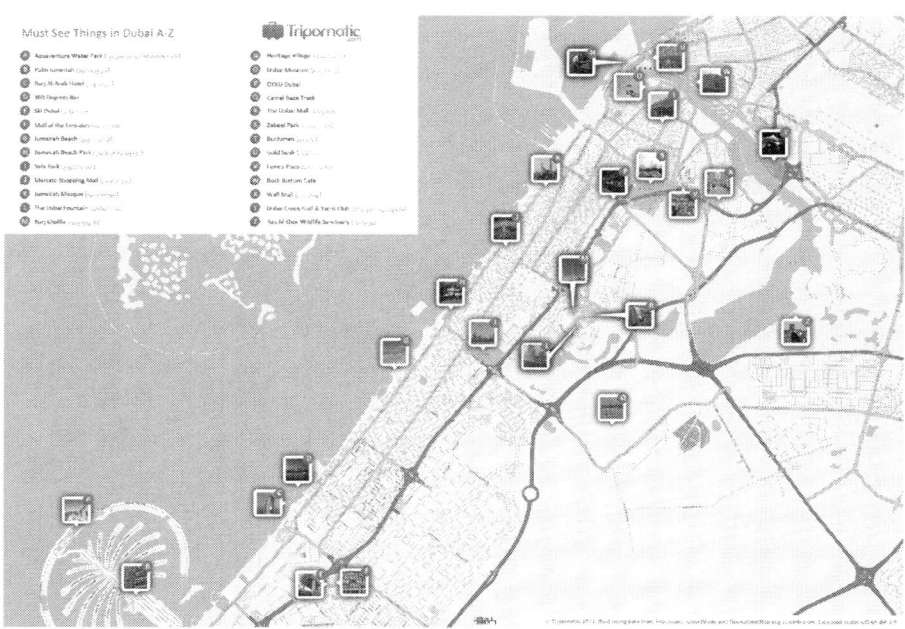

Discover Dubai

Dubai is cleverly marketed as one of the most luxurious and expensive destinations in the world but don't despair, this guide will show you how to ignore the marketing and how to luxuriate on a budget but first a bit of history.

Dubai wasn't always a super-car traffic jam on a big-city street with towering skyscrapers. Nomadic cattle herders were the first Dubai settlers, setting up camp here in 3000 BCE. In 1833, Al Maktoum of the Bani Yas tribe captured Dubai and Dubai became an independent emerate. In December 1971 the United Arab Emirates where formed after Britain left the Persian Gulf.

In 1966 everything changed when oil was discovered in Dubai Sheikh Rashid utilized the oil money to develop Dubai. This is still ongoing, today one out of every 4 cranes in the world is located in Dubai. Dubai's artificial Palm Islands use enough sand to fill 2.5 Empire State Buildings. And expats make up 85% of the population.

The trick to keeping your trip affordable is to get off the tourist track and find the local deals. If you follow the advice we have outlined in this guide you could definitely get away with having the time of your life on $40 a day.

Planning your trip

The cheapest time to visit

There are fewer crowds and pleasant temperatures between mid-November and early December, and again during the first half of March. Dubai in the summer months is unbearably hot.

One thing to remember is that The weekend is Friday and Saturday. People work on Sundays.

Where to stay

Stay near Burj Khalifa (Dubai's Downtown), Jumeirah Beach, Dubai Marina or The Palm Jumeirah. All have easy connections to get around and great views.

The cheapest place to stay

If you're travelling solo hostels are your best option, both for meeting people and saving pennies. Backpacker 16 Hostel isn't in the centre but is close to the metro and is at $13 a night will be the best bang for your buck.

Due to the volume of business travellers it is difficult to find good discounts on hotels but three star Signature Hotel Al Barsha consistently offer a room for two for around $35 a night, and it has good transport links to attractions because we were two people we chose to stay here.

Airbnb private rooms in downtown average around $50 a night, so check hostels or hotel rooms first.

Get a five-star hotel on a hostel budget

Booking.com drop prices for many under capacity five-star hotels in the hopes you will spend money at their restaurants/ mini-bars etc. This only works in low-season or when there aren't many visitors in town for whatever reason. Check on the day you want to stay and book. I stayed at the five star Canal Central Hotel for $16 using this method and many others around the globe. Just remember it normally only works for two-nights and only on SAME DAY bookings.

How to enjoy a $1,000 trip to Dubai for $220

(full breakdown at the end of the guide)

Stay	Signature Hotel Al Barsha $30 a night (with a five star supplement stay)
Eat	Average meal cost: $6 - $12
Move	Dubai Metro and local taxi's
See	Entrance to the tallest building in the world $34
Total	US$220

Exchange Rate

Amount

1

From

USD
US Dollar

To

AED
Emirati Dirham

1 USD =

3.67250 AED

1 AED = 0.272294 USD
1 USD = 3.67250 AED

US Dollar to Emirati Dirham Conversion

Last updated: 2019-01-20 15:51 UTC

All figures are live mid-market rates, which are not available to consumers and are for informational purposes only. To see the rates we quote for money transfer, please select Live Money Transfer Rates.

FF

Unique bargains I love in Dubai

It is definitely not known as the land of bargains but there are quite a few if you look closely. Miracle garden is a wonderful flower garden that's just $12 to see 72,000 square metres of beautiful flowers and it has a butterfly house. The shopping centers, although not historical have a lot of cool installations to check out and they're free or Head to Global village, a huge outdoor market for people that come from over the world, bargain down the prices.

Every Tuesday night is Ladies night and most bars do free drinks for girls and deals on food. Plenty of beaches to go to for free.

Regular taxis are cheaper than Uber, just make sure they put on the meter and repeat your destination.

And there are plenty of restaurants and small cafeterias that you can eat in cheaply (a few dollars) around Bur Dubai and Deira.

One tip: If you're female, keep a pashmina in your bag its handy for visiting mosques and the shopping centres (where aircon is reeved to artic conditions).

How to use this book

Google and tripadvisor are your on-the-go guides while travelling, a travel guide adds the most value during the planning phase and maybe if you're without wifi, as a reference when travelling (always download the google map for your destination - having an offline map will make using this guide much easier). So for ease of use we've set the book out the way you travel starting with arriving, how to get around, then on to the money-saving tips. We prioritised the tips by how much money you can save and then by how likely it was that you would be able to find the tip alone with a google search. Meaning those we think you could find alone are nearer the bottom. I hope you find this layout useful. If you have any ideas about making super cheap guides easy to use, please email me philgattang@gmail.com .Now let's started with juicing the most pleasure from your trip with the least money.

OUR SUPER CHEAP TIPS...

Arriving

You can get from Dubai Airport to the city center by metro for around $2.

Getting around

The Dubai metro is fast, clean and inexpensive. Buy a Nol Red card for 2 AED with 45 credit $10 and it should get you around for a week.

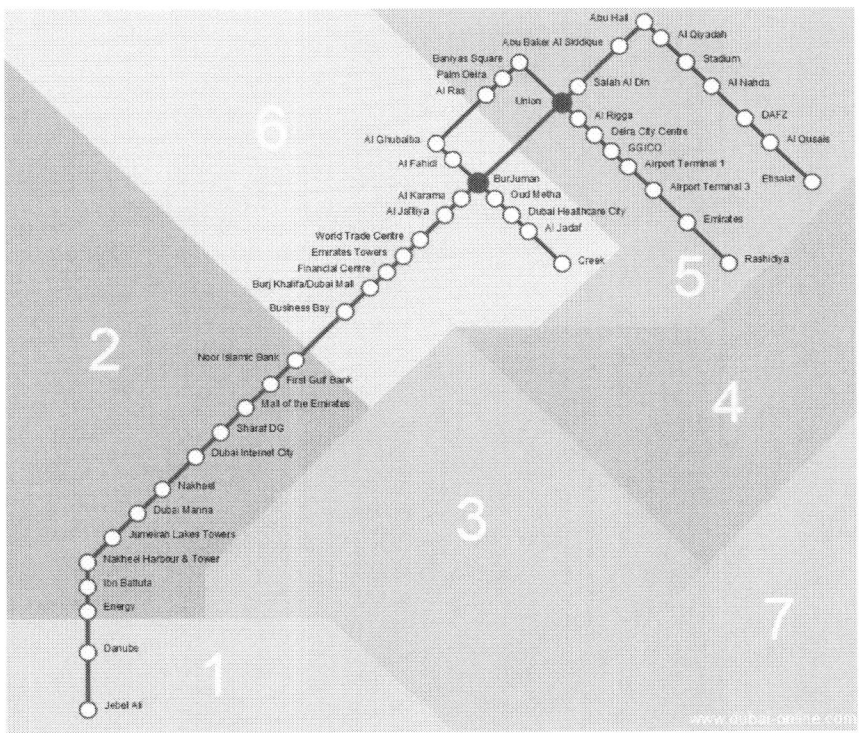

Taxi's are very cheap and very useful in Dubai's scorching heat, always make sure your driver puts the meter on and confirms your destination.

Start with a free walking tour

Forget exploring the city by wandering around aimlessly. Start with a free organised tour. Nothing compares to local advice, especially when travelling on a budget. Ask for their recommendations for the best cheap eats, the best bargains, the best markets, the best place for a particular street eat. Perhaps some of it will be repeated from this guide, but it can't hurt to ask, especially if you have specific needs or questions. At the end you should leave an appropriate tip (usually around $5), but nobody bats an eye if you are unable or unwilling to do so, tell them you will leave a good review and always give them a little gift from home - I always carry small Vienna fridge magnets and I always tip the $5, but it is totally up to you.

This is the free tour I did. I thought it was a great introduction to Dubai and it covered all the main attractions and helped us get our bearings. You can book here: https://freetoursbyfoot.com/dubai-tours/

A note on paying for tours

The only time paying for a tour is worth it, is when you couldn't reach the place without the tour (e.g you need a boat), or when the tour is about the same price as the attraction entry. Otherwise you can do a range of self-guided tours using gpsmycity.com for FREE.

FREE Attractions

Go to see the **choreographed dancing Dubai Fountain at Dubai Mall**, with the Burj Khalifa as a rising backdrop. The Dubai Mall itself is filled with attractions, most famously the Dubai Aquarium (free peeks from inside the mall) and a giant dinosaur skeleton.

The iconic **Burj Al Arab** looks great from Sunset Beach or Madinat Jumeirah - and costs nothing to admire.

Wander around **Masdar City** For close-ups of futuristic sustainable architecture.

Al Bastakiya is a Historic district of pre-modern Dubai and an area of traditional-style buildings once inhabited by the local ruling family. worth a wander.

Dubai is an international city with tons of expats with lots of free time ready to do lots of things. That means lots of MeetUp groups and Facebook communities organising events - a lot of them for free. Make friends with expats, just don't take everything they say about Dubai seriously. meetup.com/dubai

Waterfront Strolls

For scenic and instagram worthy photos walk from Dubai Creek to Al Ghubaiba metro station to the Al Fahidi Historic District Watch the wooden abras (water taxis) and neon dhows (traditional wooden boat) set sail for Iran and Sudan.

Make your way to the new Dubai Water Canal (opened in 2016) for a waterside walk with one of the best view. With more than 3.2km of promenade its a great place to snap Dubai's ever-evolving skyline.

See how the Bedouins Lived

Dubai is unrecognisable from its desert beginnings. An afternoon desert safari with a 4WD dune-drive and Arabic dinner under the stars can be booked for AED125 (US$34) with dinner and all transfers included. You'll get a taste of Bedouin life and be home in your hotel by 10pm. This is the tour we did, and it was the highlight of our trip: https://www.viator.com/tours/Dubai/Desert-Safari-from-Dubai-Including-Entertainment-and-Activities/d828-34459P15

Visit the WORLD'S TALLEST BUILDING

Experience the architectural engineering feats that make the city what it is today by visiting the world's tallest building: Burj Khalifa stands at more than 828 metres high. Tickets to 'At The Top', the observation deck are $34 per person. It is cheaper to book on the site (30 days in advance) https://www.burjkhalifa.ae/en/

Beach day + free yoga

Go to Dubai's beaches for free including Al Mamzar, Kite Beach, Sunset Beach and JBR Beach. JBR Beach offers **free yoga several mornings a week.** For more free yoga check out https://www.meetup.com/topics/free-yoga-classes/ae/dubai/

Wild Wadi Waterpark on the cheap

Go to Wild Wadi Waterpark at 4pm and you'll pay $20 instead of the regular $40 as prices are lowered two hours before the 6pm closing time, if you're just looking for a quick cool-down on the cheap this is it.

Jumeirah Mosque

Mosques in the UAE are generally closed to non-Muslims, which is why it's such a privilege to Admire the beauty of the Jumeirah Mosque on guided tours costing a mere Dhs20 just $5.

During the 75-minute guided tour, you'll learn about the Islamic culture and history of the region. You are encouraged to ask questions. Jumeirah Mosque is open six days per week for non-Muslims (all except Fridays), with tours at 10am. All visitors must wear long pants or skirts, and long sleeves and women need a scarf to cover their hair.

The Best Souks

Dubai's Souks are a fun and eye-opening plunge into local culture and, unless you succumb to the persistent vendors, it will cost you nothing. If you're interested in making a purchase, start off the bargaining process by offering half the quoted price. Here are some unique things to buy:

- Camel Milk Chocolate.
- Dubai Dates (Dried Fruits)
- Arabic Attars (Perfume Oil)
- Pashmina Shawls.
- Coffee and Arabic Coffee Pot

Dubai's flea market is one the cheaper markets in Dubai.
Address: Gate # 1 2 & 3, Zabeel Park,Zabeel
Closes 11PM

Or you can head to Bur Dubai and explore the modern Al Seef shopping district before jumping on a traditional abra boat, where for AED1 (US$0.27), you can take a short trip across the bustling Dubai Creek - a waterway that is the heart of Old Dubai. Disembark in Deira for the spice, textile and gold souks; The Spice souk is adjacent to the Dubai Gold Souk. The gold in Dubai is of exceptional quality and value, but it is a wonderful experience to simply window-shop. It's best to visit in the afternoon, when the souks come alive with activity.

Other more modern souks (and more expensive) worth exploring include: Meena Bazaar. The Friday Market. Fruit & Vegetable Souk. Naif Souk. Karama Market. Souk Madinat Jumeirah, Souk Al Bahar (in Downtown Dubai) and Khan Murjan (in Dubai Wafi City).

Cool off in Malls

Dubai has about 65 malls catering to its 3 million people. There's a faux-Venetian Mercato Mall, and the ornate Ibn Battuta Mall, modeled on a famous Moroccan Berber explorer. Here are the best ones to visit:

- The Dubai Mall. This is the most visited mall in Dubai.
- mall of the Emirates. Mall of the Emirates is home to Ski Dubai.
- Dubai Festival City Mall.
- Ibn Battuta Mall.

- City Centre Mirdif.
- City Centre Deira.
- Burjuman Centre.
- Mercato Shopping Mall.

Food halls in each are pretty cheap, but shopping bargains are better had in the souks.

Zabeel Park

The most central park is Zabeel Park, which has lush flora, a lake and the new Dubai Frame observation tower and is free to enter.

Street Art

Thanks to the Dubai Street Museum project Dubai has gotten more artful graffiti . Large-scale murals celebrating the UAE's history fill entire walls on 2nd December St in Satwa. And the Al Fahidi Historic District in Bur Dubai are home to some of the best street art in Dubai.

Gallery Hop

Head to Alserkal Avenue in industrial Al Quoz or Gate Village at the Dubai International Finance Centre to look at local art in galleries for free.

The Al Fahidi Historical Neighbourhood is also full of art galleries and courtyard cafés that feel like a world away from the ultra-modern city.

XVA Gallery and Majlis Gallery are the best we visited in the city.

Majlis Gallery.

Workout for free

Many high-end gyms around Dubai offer trials complete with free access to sauna's, steam rooms and pools. Fitness first has a couple of branches with a free trial day, just claim yours here: https://uae.fitnessfirstme.com/try-us

I wouldn't mention anything about travelling through. They are offering you the pass for free to convert you into a paying member. Don't feel bad, think of all the money you've paid gyms and never used their services. You can also leave them a review online if you feel bad for using their facilities for free. Here's a list of 10 more high-end gyms with free days - 10 high-end gyms in Dubai you can try for free - Gulf Business https://gulfbusiness.-com/revealed-10-high-end-gyms-dubai-can-try-free

Enjoy high tea at a seven star hotel

First off, this is not super cheap, but it is a cheaper hack. Burj Al Arab Jumeirah is the world's only seven-star hotel. It is worth seeing from outside, but unless you are a guest you aren't allowed inside. For $150USD per person you can reserve for afternoon tea. It is is served in seven courses. With that you receive unlimited coffee, tea, scones, finger sandwiches, pastries, etc. The menu starts with a glass of Louis Roederer champagne and the **$150 though insanely steep is a fraction of the $1,835** per night you'd have to pay to stay here for one night. High tea is served at the Skyview Bar located on the top floor of the sail-shaped hotel.

The Lost Chambers Aquarium $31

It's one of the most visited and one of the cheaper attractions in Dubai. This Atlantis-themed aquarium with underwater halls & tunnels housing marine life, plus feeding sessions. Check www.groupon.ae for discount tickets.

Go to the Races for free

Go to Meydan Racecourse to watch some of the world's finest thoroughbreds and most famous jockeys. The state-of-the art stadium is impressive in itself and the vibe can be electric. And will only cost you the metro and taxi fare there.

You can try out Al Marmoum for camel racing. It's just south of Dubai and the experience is quintessentially Arabic.

Food and drinks tips

Free drinks refills

If you need a laptop day head to Fatburger in Dubai Mall with free coffee and soft drink refills.

2nd of December Street

Known as Al Dhiyafa Street this buzzing street is the place to load your plate cheaply with cuisines from India, Iran, Lebanon and more. Dubai's best chicken shawarmas at Al Mallah, served in a bread pocket with salty pickles and garlic but bring cash – most places don't take cards.

Happy Hour & Ladies' Nights

Offered by many bars throughout the week. Most cafes, restaurants, spas, bars and malls offer free wifi for their customers. Free public wi-fi requires a local number for registration.

Not super cheap but worth the fee if you want to go...

Aquaventure Waterpark - $94
Waterslides, zip line circuit & beach
Vast water park with zip lines, slides through shark-filled lagoons & a splash area for kids. The price is lowered two hours before the park closes if you're just looking for a quick cool-down on the cheap.

Legoland Dubai - $94
Amusement park, bollywood, and water park
Legoland Dubai is a theme park that opened on October 31, 2016. It is the first Legoland park in the Middle East and the seventh in the world. The park was originally scheduled to open in 2011

Don't leave without seeing (even if only from outside)

Burj Khalifa
Spired 828-meter skyscraper with a viewing deck, restaurant, hotel and offices and 11-hectare park.

Burj Al Arab Jumeirah
Opulent hotel featuring ornate suites, plus 9 restaurants, 4 pools, a private beach & a luxe spa.

The Dubai Mall
Huge shopping and leisure centre, with department stores, plus an ice rink, aquarium and a cinema.

Palm Islands
Palm Islands are three artificial islands, Palm Jumeirah, Deira Island and Palm Jebel Ali, on the coast of Dubai, United Arab Emirates. Creation of the islands started in 2001. As of November. It uses enough sand to fill the empire state building four times over.

Palm Jumeirah
The tree-shaped Palm Jumeirah island is known for glitzy hotels, posh apartment towers and upmarket global restaurants. Food trucks offering snacks like shawarma dot the Palm Jumeirah Boardwalk

Dubai Marina
Dubai Marina is an affluent residential neighborhood known for The Beach at JBR, a leisure complex with al fresco dining and sandy stretches to relax on. Smart cafes and pop-up craft markets

Mall of the Emirates
Huge shopping mall with international department stores, a ski centre and a multi-screen cinema.

Dubai Creek
Dubai Creek is a saltwater creek located in Dubai, United Arab Emirates. Previously it extended to Ras Al Khor Wildlife Sanctuary but as part of the new Dubai canal it extends through to the

The Dubai Fountain
Massive fountain with 30-minute displays of water jets reaching 140 m, set to a music & light show.

Wild Wadi Water Park
Aquatic roller coasters & surfing wave machine in outdoor water park with pools, slides & tunnels.

Ski Dubai
Indoor ski center with a mountain motif & snow for year-round skiing & snowboarding.

Madinat Jumeirah
Upscale hotel resort with private beach

Upmarket resort complex with 5 hotels, a modern souk, restaurants & bars, plus a private beach.

Dubai Gold Souk
Marked by a wooden arch, this bustling bazaar features many stores selling dazzling gold jewellery.

Jumeirah Beach
Bustling, public urban beach backed by high-rise hotels, with a children's playground & BBQ areas.

The World
The World or The World Islands is an artificial archipelago of various small islands constructed in the rough shape of a world map, located in the waters of the Persian Gulf, 4.0 kilometres off

Al Bastakiya
Area of traditional-style buildings in typical materials housing arts & cultural exhibits & museums.

Aquaventure Waterpark - $94
Vast water park with zip lines, slides through shark-filled lagoons & a splash area for kids.

Jumeirah Mosque
Landmark mosque with guided tours offered to non-Muslims to promote cultural understanding.

Jumeirah Beach Hotel

Upscale beachfront property with 6 pools, a diving centre & a spa, plus 20 restaurants & bars.

Dubai Spice Souk

Dubai Spice Souk or the Old Souk is a traditional market in Dubai, United Arab Emirates. The Spice Souk is located in eastern Dubai, in Deira and is adjacent to the Dubai Gold Souk. The Spice

The Lost Chambers Aquarium

Atlantis-themed aquarium with underwater halls & tunnels housing marine life, plus feeding sessions.

Grand Mosque

Muslim place of worship built in 1900
This mosque accommodates 1200 worshippers & allows non-Muslim visitors in the minaret only.

Emirates Towers

The Emirates Towers is a building complex in Dubai that contains the Emirates Office Tower and Jumeirah Emirates Towers Hotel. The two towers, which rise to 355 m and 309 m, respectively, stand

Dubai Miracle Garden

The Dubai Miracle Garden is a flower garden located in the district of Dubailand, Dubai, United Arab Emirates. The garden was launched on Valentine's Day in 2013. The garden occupies over 72,000

Jumeirah Emirates Towers Hotel

High-end hotel with chic dining & a spa
Upscale hotel with polished rooms & stylish restaurants, plus a luxe spa & shopping.

Dubai Aquarium & Underwater Zoo - AED 55
High-tech marine family attraction
Underwater tunnel under a huge shark- & ray-filled tank, plus a creepy crawly zone with snakes.

Safa Park
Public park with a boating lake
Green, public space with sports pitches, bike rental, BBQ areas & a boating lake.

IMG Worlds of Adventure - $77.61
Sprawling indoor theme park with rides
Large indoor amusement park offering rides, eateries & shows with Cartoon Network & Marvel themes.

Saeed Al Maktoum House
House museum with historic artifacts
Grand, 19th-century home of a former ruler of Dubai, now a museum displaying historic memorabilia.

Al Mamzar Beach Park
Beach park with cabin rentals, swimming pools & restaurant plus children's games & bicycle hire.

Deira Island
Deira Island is a group of artificial islands in Dubai, United Arab Emirates. The project was initially planned to be part of the Palm Islands and was called Palm Deira.

Creek Side Park
Lush waterside park with swimming pool, kids' play areas, a cable car, amphitheater & restaurants.

Bluewaters Island
Bluewaters Island is a development project under construction 500 metres off the Jumeirah Beach Residence coastline, near Dubai Marina, in Dubai, United Arab Emirates. The project was approved

Palm Jebel Ali
The Palm Jebel Ali is an artificial archipelago in Dubai, United Arab Emirates which began construction in October 2002, was originally planned to be completed by mid-2008 and has been on hold

Mushrif Park
Vast public space with a swimming pool, green areas, horse & camel rides, plus a 500-seat theater.

Al Ras
Al Oqaili Museum & traditional markets
Part of Dubai's old Deira district, Al Ras owes its traditional vibe to long-standing markets like the Gold Souk, selling ornate jewelry, and the aromatic Spice Souk. The narrow streets hold

Is the tap water drinkable?

It is safe to drink but contaminants from the pipes leading to homes and offices may affect the taste, so stick to filtered water if in doubt.

Haggle-o-meter

How much can you save haggling here?

You can save a lot by haggling in Dubai. Start low and work your way up with humour. When you walk away, the person you're haggling with, will call you back, and this is when you will get the lowest price.

Role play: If you're with a friend, ask them to role play with you, to convince you to buy it, that they are the side of the seller will increase your chances of getting a good price.

Haggling doesn't mean you are angry or hostile, sparking confrontation. In fact, this can have the effect of making the seller less flexible. Approach with a warm, friendly nature, with the idea that you both want to win - the seller wants to make a sale and you want the lovely item at a great price. If you build a bit of rapport this makes the seller much more open to you.

Download the language packet for Arabic before you go on _Google translate_. You will need to install the app and then you'll be able to translate anything even if you don't

have wifi. It has a camera function too, which can be par-
ticularly useful for eating at local restaurants.

Enjoy your first Day for under $30

Start your day with some window shopping at Mall of emirates and watch the surreal people skiing at Ski Dubai – an indoor snow park with the world's only indoor black diamond ski run. Then take the metro and a taxi to Burj Khalifa- the tallest building in the world. Next Go to Burj Al Arab, the world's only seven-star hotel for your unless you want to pay for $150 for the Sky Tea just snap some photos from outside. Next door you can go to Wild Wadi Waterpark at 4pm for a cheap visit to the waterpark.

Next, take the monorail to Atlantis Hotel at Palm Jumeirah- a man-made island in the shape of a palm tree you can look at the aquarium without having to pay to go into Lost Chambers.

Return to Time Cafe for a night of lively and cheap drinks. You can get a beverage for Dhs30 or less here.

Websites to save you Money

1. **TalkTalkbnb.com -** Here you stay for free when you teach the host your native language
2. Rome2Rio.com - the go to site for good travel prices on train, bus, planes etc. Especially good for paths less travelled.
3. couchsurfing.com - stay for free with a local - always check reviews.
4. trustedhousesitter.com - always check reviews
5. booking.com - now sends you vouchers for discounts in the city when you book through them
6. blablacar.com - travel in car with locals already going to your destination
7. airbnb.com for both accommodation and experiences.
8. hostelbookers.com - book hostels
9. https://freetoursbyfoot.com/dubai-tours/ - free tours
10. https://www.groupon.ae/ - check for deals on Dubai attractions.

Need to Know

Currency: United Arab Emirates Dirham

Language: Arabic

Money: Widely available ATMs and card is widely accepted.

Visas: http://www.doyouneedvisa.com/

Time: GMT + 4

Important Numbers

999

Watch to understand the History

Dubai 's history is fascinating. There are tons of documentaries. This is a 5 minute one that gives you a good overview - https://www.youtube.com/watch?v=1AmOZhGpcFo

Cheapest route to Dubai from America

At the time of writing Norwegian are flying to Dubai for the lowest fare. NOTE: it is $200 cheaper to buy single tickets. I specialise in finding cheap flights, so if you need help finding a cheap flight simply review this book and send me an email.
philgtang@gmail.com

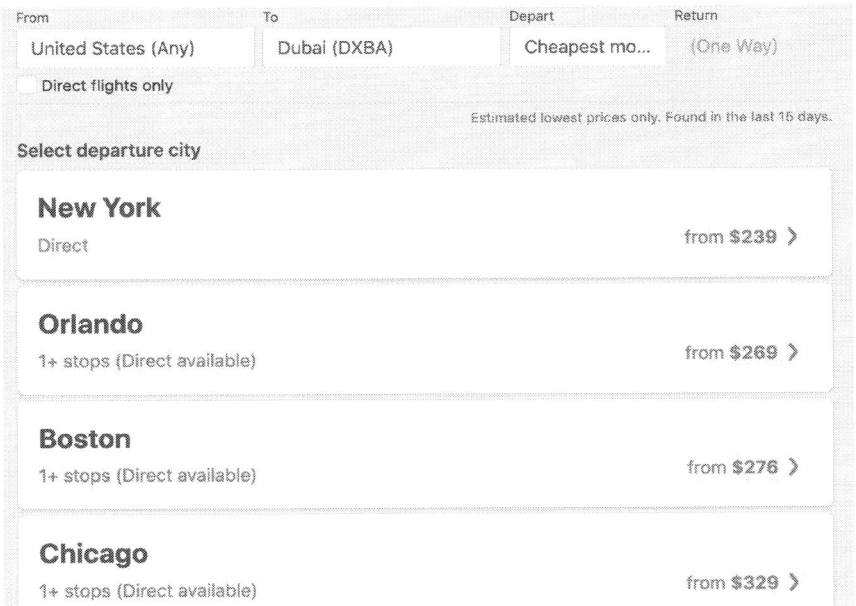

Cheapest route to Dubai from Europe

At the time of writing Wizz Air are flying very cheaply to the Dubai from Budapest for $188 roundtrip. Be careful with cheap airlines, most will allow **hand-luggage only**, and some charge for anything that is not a backpack. Check their websites before booking if you need to take luggage.

I specialise in finding cheap flights, so if you need help finding a cheap flight simply review this book and send me an email. philgtang@gmail.com

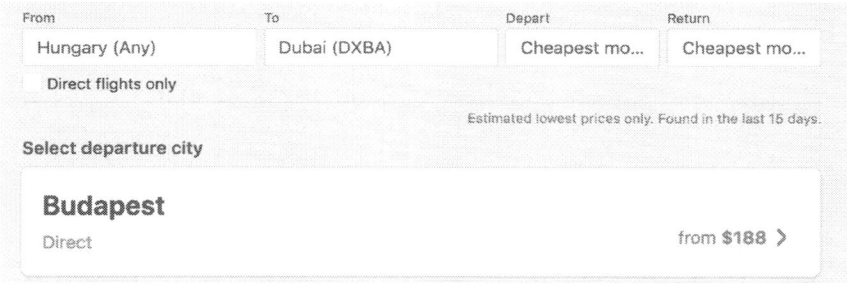

Cheap Eats

Many Emirati dishes include camel as one of their main ingredients. Stuffed camel is a famous dish in Dubai. Lamb and mutton are the more favored meats, then goat and beef. Popular beverages are coffee and tea, which can be supplemented with cardamom, saffron, or mint to give it a distinct flavour. Dubai is home to a lot of overpriced restaurants, so check the menu before sitting down.

You can fill your stomach without emptying your wallet at these restaurants with mains under $10.

(Download the offline map on google maps, (instructions 1. go to app 2. select offline apps in the left sidebar 3. go to the area you want to download 4. click download). Then simply type the restaurant names in to navigate)

Ravi Restaurant
Pakistani
This popular, unassuming eatery dishes up an array of traditional Pakistani & Indian fare.
Late-night food · Casual · Vegetarian options

Yalla Momos
Fast Food
Relaxed restaurant serving Tibetan momo dumplings to eat in and take away.If you're craving momos on the cheap, this is the place to be.

Scots American Grill
Cosy · Vegetarian options · Groups
Opens 6PM
Steaks are excellent and affordable.

Afghan Kebab House
Excellent kebabs at low prices.

Wokyo™ Noodle Bar
Asian Fusion
Cosy · Casual · Good for kids
Really quick service, simple menu with a lot of choice, good food.

Ponderosa Steakhouse U.A.E.
Old West-themed chain known for its steaks, chicken & all-you-can-eat buffet. They have lots of food variety for an affordable price.

Dubai Fish Hut - Oud Metha
A must visit and the food is delicious and price is cheap for the quality and portions.

Al Ustad Special Kabab
Persian
Popular spot turning out kebabs & other Persian favorites in an easygoing, photo-filled space. Food was excellent and cheap, at around 70 AED for 2 people.

Canara Restaurant
Good n cheap food..excellent for fish

Calicut Paragon Restaurant
Casual restaurant for mainly South Indian dishes with a focus on seafood and wide vegetarian choice.
Casual · Vegetarian options · Good for kids

Islam in practice

Islam is the official religion of Dubai and the United Arab Emirates. It is one of the most liberal places in the Middle East and followers of other religions (except Judaism) are tolerated. Visitors should respect Islam and Arabic culture and laws.

Clothing: In practice most expats in Dubai dress as they would if they were in Europe but unless at the beach women should not wear short shorts or other revealing garments

Public displays of affection: Holding hands is fine for married couples, but kissing or hugging in public are not acceptable. So if you're married its fine to hold hands, if you're unmarried keep any touching inside the hotel or hostel.

Swearing: Dubai is very conservative when it comes to bad language do not swear in public. You should avoid 'losing face' so don't argue in public.

Photos: Don't take photographs of government buildings or of people without their permission.

As long as you are considerate, you will have no problems.

Getting Out

Bus

You can take the buses from Dubai to Abu Dhabi for 5 AED. The bus takes 1.40 hours and leaves from Ibn Battuta Metro Station 4.

Plane

At the time of writing Wizz Air are offering the cheapest flights onward.Take advantage of discounts and specials. Sign up for e-newsletters from local carriers including Wizz Air to learn about special fares. Be careful with cheap airlines, most will allow hand-luggage only, and some charge for anything that is not a back-

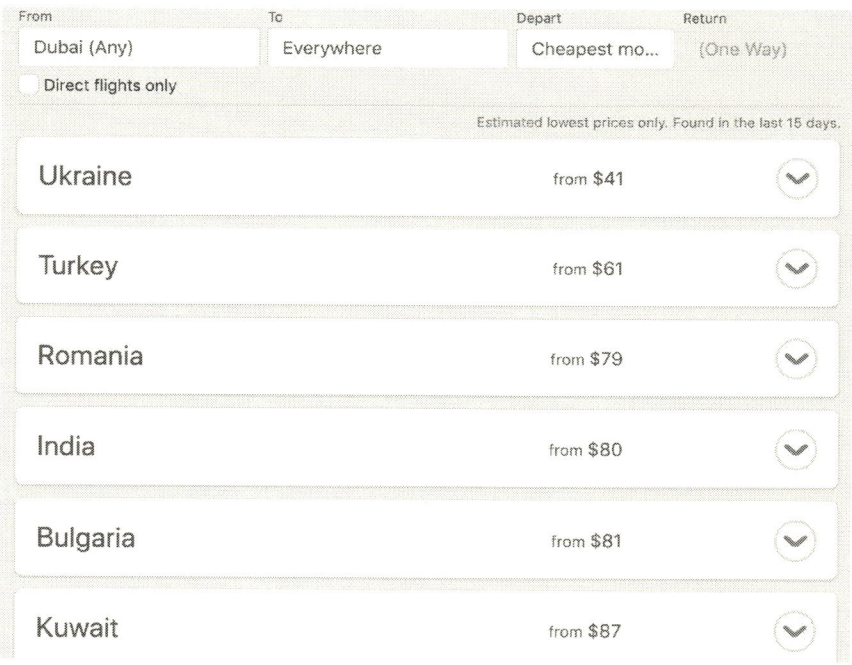

pack. Check their websites before booking if you need to take luggage.

Personal Cost Break-down

	How	Cost normally	Cost when following suggested tip
How I got from the city	Metro	$25 Taxi	$2
Where I stayed	Hotel $30 a night		$90 split between two people so $45 each.
Tastiest street foods I ate and cost	Kebabs	Meals come in around $10 average.	$10 average
How I got around	Metro and taxi's. Not all attractions are close to the metro, so pick up local taxi's.	Regular taxi's are 30% cheaper than ubers.	We took two taxi's everyday in Dubai during a three day stay and paid $15
What I saw and paid	Beaches, tallest building, souks, mosques, galleries,	I paid to visit the desert and the water park.	$60
My onward flight	Kiev	$200	$41
My Total costs	US$170		US$220

Print or screenshot for easy reference

	How	Cost
Get from the airport	metro	$2
Stay	Hotel for 3 days	$90
Food	Average meal cost: $10 - see cheap eats section.	$10 per meal
Get around	Metro	$8 for all rides
See	Desert, world's tallest building, aquarium, Atlantis palm hotel, beaches, street art and galleries	$60
Best discounts	Groupon offers up to 70% off attractions in Dubai	n/a
Get out	Onward flight to Kiev	$41
Total	US$220	$220

PRACTICAL THINGS TO REMEMBER TO SAVE MONEY

- Buy a Nol red Card before using the metro, local bus, tram or water bus.
- Download google maps for for use offline, this will save you on having to use a taxi, if the weather is cooler you can walk.
- Have a game plan for buying things at the souks and haggle!
- Bring a water-to-go bottle or similar to filter your water
- Show respect during Ramadan by not eating in front of those fasting.
- No public displays of affection if you and your partner are un-married (fines are upwards of 500AED).
- Look on Groupon.ae for deals on visiting attractions and restaurants.

Things to watch out for

Crime is rare in Dubai. Petty crime, such as purse snatching and pickpocketing are a risk in crowds and at the souks. Don't keep anything in your back pockets.

Dubai has among the highest incidences of accidents and road fatalities in the world, be careful when walking.

The Gulf waters may look harmless on the surface, but under currents can be very strong so use caution in the water and if in doubt stay near shore.

The secret to saving HUGE amounts of money when travelling to Dubai is...

Your mindset. Money is an emotional topic, if you associate words like skinflint , cheapskate , Miser (and its £9.50 to go into Charles Dickens London house) with being thrifty when travelling you are likely to say 'F-it' and spend your money needlessly because you associate pain with saving money. You spend now for an immediate reward. Our brains are prehistoric they focus on surviving day to day. Travel companies and hotels know this and put trillions into making you believe you will be happier when you spend on their products or services. Our poor brains are up against outdated programming and an onslaught of advertisements bombarding us with the message: spending money on travel equals PLEASURE. To correct this carefully lodged propaganda in your frontal cortex you simply need to imagine your future self.

Saving money does not make you a cheapskate. It makes you smart. How do people get rich? They invest their money. They don't go out and earn it, they let their money earn more money. So every time you want to spend money, imagine this: while you travel your money is working for you, not you for money. While you sleep the money you've invested is going up and up. That's a pleasure a pricey entrance fee can't give you. Thinking about putting your money to work for you tricks your brain into believing you are not withholding pleasure from yourself, you are saving your money to invest so you can go to even more amazing places. Thus turning thrifty travel into a pleasure filled sport.

When you've got money invested - If you want to splash your cash on a first-class airplane seat - you can. I can't tell you how to invest your money, only that you should. Saving $20 on taxi's doesn't seem like much but overtime you could be saving upwards of $15,000 a year, which is a deposit for a house which you can rent on Airbnb to finance more travel. Your brain making money looks like your brain on cocaine so tell yourself saving money is making money.

Scientists have proved that imagining your future self is the easiest way to associate pleasure with saving money. You can download FaceApp — which will give you a picture of what you will look like older and greyer, or you can simply take a deep breath just before spending money and ask yourself if you will regret the purchase later.

The easiest ways to waste money travelling are:

1. Getting a taxi. The solution to this is to always download the google map before you go. Many taxi drivers will drive you around for 15 minutes when the place you were trying to get to is a 5 minute walk… remember while not getting an overpriced taxi to tell yourself, 'I am saving money to free myself for more travel.' but in Dubai if temperatures are high, it is worth to pay a little not to walk. Heat exhaustion will cost you more, and local taxi's are cheap.
2. Spending money on overpriced food when hungry. The solution: carry snacks. A banana and an apple will cost you, in most places less than a dollar.
3. Spending on entrance fees to top rated attractions. If you really want to do it, spend the money happily. If you're conflicted sleep on it. I don't regret spending $200 on a skydive over the Great Barrier Reef, I do regret going to the top of the shard in London for $60. Only you can know but make sure its your decision and not the marketing directors at said top-rated attraction.
4. Telling yourself 'you only have the chance to see/eat/ experience it now'. While this might be true, make sure YOU WANT to spend the money. Money spent is

money you can't invest and often you can have the same experience for much less.

You can experience luxurious travel on a small budget which will trick your brain into thinking you're already a high-roller, which will mean you'll be more likely to start acting like one and invest your money. Stay in five-star hotels for $5 by booking on the day of your stay on booking.com to enjoy last minute deals. You can go to fancy restaurants using daily deal sites. Ask your airline about last minute upgrades to first-class or business. I paid $100 extra on a $179 ticket to Cuba from Germany to be bumped to Business Class. When you ask you will be surprised what you can get both at hotels and airlines.

Travel, as the saying goes is the only thing you spend money on that makes you richer. In practice, you can easily waste money, making it difficult to enjoy that metaphysical wealth. The biggest money saving secret is to turn bargain hunting into a pleasurable activity, not an annoyance. Budgeting consciously can be fun, don't feel disappointed because you don't spend the $60 to go into an attraction, feel good because soon that $60 will soon be earning money for you. Meaning, you'll have the time and money to enjoy more metaphysical wealth, while your bank balance increases.

So there it is, you can stay stay in nice hotels, and enjoy tours and all the sights for just over $200 - all by being strategic with your trip planning. None of these less expensive recommended options sacrifices much quality compared to the more expensively priced alternative.

We've arranged everything in the guide to offer the best bang for your buck. Which means we took the view that if it's not a good investment for your money we wouldn't include it. Why would a guide called 'Super Cheap' include lots of overpriced attractions? That said, if you think we've missed something or have unanswered questions just ping me an email philgtang@gmail.com I'm on central Europe time and normally reply within 8 hours of getting your mail.

Don't put your dreams off!

Time is a currency you never get back and travel is its greatest return on investment. Plus now you know you can visit Dubai for a fraction of the price most would have you believe.

Metro Map

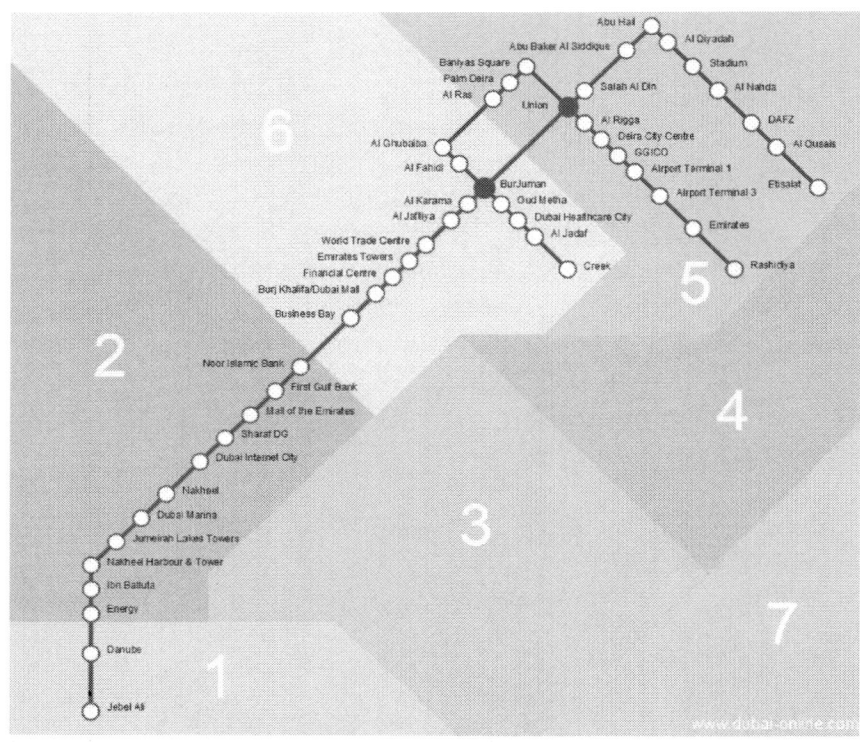

Thank you for reading

Dear Reader,

If you have found this book useful please consider writing a short review on Amazon.

We pour our heart and soul into our guides, sourcing cheap tips from anyone and everyone we meet.

We are a group of four friends who all met travelling 15 years ago. We believe that great experiences don't need to blow your budget, just your mind.

I would like to ask a favour, please consider writing a short review on Amazon.

Thank you so much for reading again and for spending your time and investing your trips future in Super Cheap Guides Guides.

Phil

P.S If you need any more super cheap tips we'd love to hear from you just e-mail me at philgtang@gmail.com we have a lot of contacts in every region, so if there's a specific bargain you're hunting we can help you find it :-)

GET 300 TRAVEL GUIDES FULL OF SUPER CHEAP TIPS FREE ON AMAZON WITH KINDLE UNLIMITED.

Bonus Budget Travel Hacks

I've included these bonus travel hacks to help you plan and enjoy the trip cheaply, joyfully and smoothly.

How NOT to be ripped off

The thrill of spontaneity is incredible, but if you do a little planning ahead, you will not only save yourself from several mental troubles, but also a lot of money. I am the laziest of planners when it comes to travelling, but I make sure I begin a trip well.

1. **Never ever agree to pay as much as you want trap. Always decide on a price before.**

Whoever you're dealing with is trained to tell you, they are uninterested in money! This is a trap. If you let people do this they will ask for MUCH MORE money at the end, and because you have used there service, you will feel obliged to pay. This is a con-man's trick and nothing more.

2. Choose to stay in a hostel, instead of a hotel the first nights to get the lay of the land.

get a chance to learn so much. I have also observed that the location of hostels is often close to main attractions. Also please do not worry about luxury, you are going to spend most of your time outside anyway.

3. Pack light

You can move faster and easier. If you take heavy luggage so you will end up taking cabs which are comparatively very costly.

4. If a local approaches you, they are normally trying to scam you, this is ALWAYS true in tourist destinations.

5. Don't book for more than two days and note down the address on your phone

Unless the place you're doing is going to be busy. e.g Alaska in summer.

6. Withdraw cash from ATM's when you need it, don't carry it with you.

5. NEVER use the airport taxi service. Plan to use public transport before you reach the airport

6. Don't buy a sim card from the airport, but from the local supermarkets it will be 50% less.

7. Eat at local restaurants serving regional food
Food defines culture. Exploring all delights available to the palate.

How to overcome travel related struggles

Anxiety when flying

It has been over 40 years since a plane has been brought down because of turbulence. 40 years! Planes are built to withstand lighting strikes, extreme storms and ultimately can adjust course to get out of their way. Landing and take over are when the most accidents happen, but you have statistically three times the chance of winning a huge jackpot lottery, then you do of crashing then.

If you feel afraid on the flight focus on your breathing saying the word 'smooth' over and over until the flight is smooth. Always check the airline safety record airlinerating.com I was surprised to learn Ryanair and Easyjet as much less safe than Wizz Air according to those ratings. If there is extreme turbulence, I feel much better knowing I'm in a 7 star safety plane.

Wanting to sleep instead of seeing new places

This is a common problem. Just relax, there's little point doing fun things when you feel tired. Plan and fact in jetlag.

Going over budget

Come back from a trip to a monster credit card bill? You're not alone. These are the costs that can crept up. Don't let them.

-   To and from the airport. Solution: leave adequate time and take the cheapest method - book before.
-   Baggage. Solution: take hand luggage and post things you might need to yourself.
-   Eating out. Solution: go to cheap eats places and suggest those to friends.
-   Parking. Solution: use apps to find free parking
-   Tipping. Solution Leave a modest tip and tell the server you will write them a nice review.
-   Souvenirs. Solution: fridge magnets only.
-   Giving to the poor. (This one still gets me, but if you're giving away $10 a day - it adds up) Solution: volunteer your time at a local soup kitchens.

Price v Comfort

I love traveling, I don't love struggling. I like decent accommodation, being able to eat properly and see places and enjoy. I am never in the mood for low cost airlines or crappy transfers so here's what I do to save money.

-   Avoid organised tours unless you are going to a place where safety is a real issue. They are expensive and constrain your wanderlust to typical things. Note, I only recommend them in Algeria, Iran and Papua New Guinea - where language and gender views pose serious problems all cured by a reputable tour organiser.
-   Eat what the locals do.
-   Cook in your airbnb/ hostel where restaurants are expensive.
-   Shop at local markets.
-   Never take the first price.

- Spend time choosing your flight, and check the operator on ari-lineratings.com
- Mix up hostels and Airbnbs. Hostels for meeting people, Airbnb for relaxing and feeling 'at home'.

Not knowing where toilets are

Use Toilet Finder - https://play.google.com/store/apps/de-tails?id=com.bto.toilet&hl=en

Your airbnb is awful

Airbnb customer service is notoriously bad. Help yourself out. Never book somewhere without at least 5 reviews. Try to sort things out with the host, but if you can't take photos of everything e.g bed, bathroom, mess, doors, contact them within 24 hours and tell them you had to leave and pay for new accommodation. And ask politely for a full refund.

The airline loses your bag

Take a photo of your checked luggage before you check it.
Go to the Luggage desk before leaving the airport and report the bag missing.
Most airlines will give you an overnight bag, ask where your staying and return the bag to you within three days. Its extremely rare for them to completely lose it these days, but if that happens you should submit an insurance claim.

Your travel companion lets you down.

Whether it's a breakup or a friend cancelling, it sucks and can ramp up costs. In these cases, I normally go to a well-reviewed hostel and find someone I want to travel with - if I need someone to cover the extra costs.

Culture shock

I had one of the strongest culture shocks while spending 6 months in Japan. It was overwhelming how much I actually had to prepare when I went outside of the door (googling words and sentences what to use, where to go, which station and train line to use, what is this food called in Japanese and how does its look etc.). I was so tired constantly but in the end I just let go and went with my extremely bad Japanese. I was trying to ask for soup one day and asked for help with my piles… the people were laughing so hard one actually choked.

If you feel culture shocked its because your brain is referencing your surroundings to what you know. My tip is to just let go and learn some of the local language. You won't like everywhere you go - but you can at least relax everywhere you go.

You're tired

I feel like I just want to go go go go go and See everything and don't let myself just take some time to rest without feeling guilty or conflicted but its important to rest when travelling. I like to create a mini entertainment zone, and occasionally binge watch something or watch documentaries about where I currently am on YouTube.

Car rental

I always use carrentals.com and book with a credit card. Most credit cards will give you free insurance for the car, so you don't need to pay the extra.

You're sick

First off ALWAYS, purchase travel insurance. Including emergency transport up to $500k even to back home, which is usually less than $10 additional. I use https://www.comparethemarket.com/travel-insurance/

If I am sick I normally check into a hotel with room service and ride it out.

Make a Medication Travel Kit

Take medications with you, it is always more expensive to buy there unless you are lucky.

- Antidiarrheal medication (for example, bismuth subsalicylate, loperamide)
- Antihistamine.
- Anti-motion sickness medication.
- Medicine for pain or fever (such as acetaminophen, aspirin, or ibuprofen)
- Mild laxative.
- Cough suppressant/expectorant.
- Throat Lozenges

Save yourself from most travel related hassle

- Do not screw around with immigration and customs staff. You will lose.

- Book the most direct flight you can find, nonstop if possible. Keep weather in mind with connecting flights and watch out for connections in cities with multiple airports through different airports (airlines sometimes connect this way… watch it in places like London and New York)

- Carry a US$ 100 bill for emergency cash. I have entered a country and all ATM and credit card systems were down. US$ can be exchanged nearly anywhere in the world.

- Pack light. Pack light. Pack light. Pack light.

- On long connections, many airport lounges are pay lounges and can be very comfortable and cheaper than a transit hotel.

- Check, and recheck, required visas and such BEFORE the day of your trip. Some countries, for instance, require a ticket out of the country in order to enter. Others, like the US and Australia, require electronic authorization in advance.

- McDonalds and Starbucks offer free wifi in most of the world.

- Security is asinine and inconsistent around the world. Keep this in mind when connecting flights. Always leave at least 2 hours for international connections or international to domestic.

- Expats are rarely the best source for local information. Lots of barstool pontificates in the world.

- Wiki travel is perfect to use for a lay of the land

- Expensive luggage rarely lasts longer than cheap luggage, in my experience. Fancy leather bags are usually toast with air travel.

- Buy travel insurance. A comprehensive annual policy is best and not that expensive.

- Learning to say please and thank you in the local language is not that hard and opens doors. As does a smile and a handshake.

Where and How to Make Friends

Become popular at the airport

Want to become popular at the airport? Pack a power bar with multiple outlets and just see how many friends you make. It's amazing how many people forget their chargers, or who packed them in the luggage that they checked in!

Stay in Hostels

I note there's a line about backpacking, young, confident, hostel demographic that seems to have a whole unspoken backstory going on.

First of all, Hostels don't have to be shared dorms, and they cater to a much wider demographic than is assumed in the OP's comments. In my experience hostels were a way better environment for meeting people than hotels, and more importantly they tended to open up excursion opportunities that further opened up that opportunity. Hotel guests tend to be more cocooned, either couples or families, or if solo, more often than not business travellers, who are rarely interested in chit-chat.

Or take up a hobby

However, if hostels are a definite no-no; find an interest. Take up a hobby where you will meet people. I've dived for years and the nature of diving is you're always paired up with a dive buddy, and I met a lot of interesting people that way. Find something like that the gets people together. However, all of this is about creating the opportunity, you still have to take it, and if you're not the most outgoing person, pack the power supply.

GENERAL HACKS

From saving space in your suitcase to scoring cheap flights, there are a wealth of travel hacks that can help you use to have a stress-free and happy travels without breaking the bank.

Planning and booking stages of travel are equally instrumental in how successful your trip will be, which can be a lot of pressure.

Before You Go

Money

- Get cash from ATMs for best rates.
- Never change at airport exchange desks unless you absolutely have to, then just change enough to get to an ATM.
- Charles Schwab High Yield Checking accounts refund every single ATM fee worldwide, require no minimum balance and have no monthly fee.
- Bring a spare credit card for real emergencies.
- Split cash in various places on your person (pockets, shoes) and in your luggage.
- Use a money belt under your clothes or put $50 in your shoe/ bra incase.

Food
-
- When it comes to food, eat in local restaurants, not tourist-geared joints or choose a hostel.
- with facilities and cook for yourself. The same goes for drinking and going out.

- Bring boiled eggs, canned tuna and nuts with you to avoid being caught out by extreme hunger and having to buy expensive/ unhealthy foods full of sugar.
- Take a spork - a knife, spoon and fork all in one.

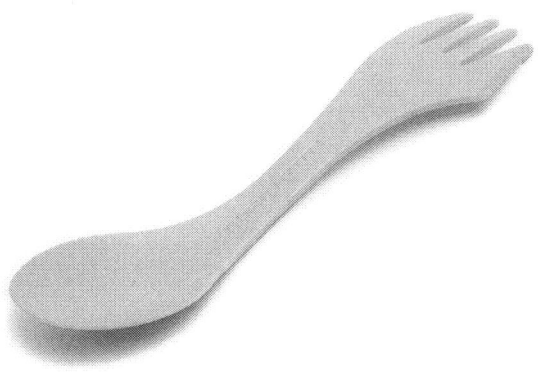

Water Bottle

Take a water bottle with a filter. We love these ones from Water to Go.
Empty it before airport security and seperate the two pieces.

Bug Sprays

Always buy on Amazon. If you have an urgent need while travelling you will pay over the odds. If you are especially tasty to mosquitoes spray your clothes with Permethrin before you travel. A 'Bite Away' zapper can be used after the bite to totally erase it. It cuts down on the itching and need for anti-hestimaines

Order free mini's

Don't buy those expensive travel sized toiletries, order travel sized freebies online. This gives you the opportunity to try brands you've never used before, and who knows, you might even find your new favourite soap.

CHEAP FLIGHT HACKS

Use skyscanner.net - they include the low-cost airlines that others like Kayak leave out.

Use open parameters, e.g if you want to fly from Chicago to Paris, put in USA to France, you may find flights from NYC to Paris for $70 and can take a cheap flight to NYC. Calculate full costs, including accommodation and getting to and from airports before bookting.

ALWAYS USE A PRIVATE BROWSER TO BOOK FLIGHTS

Skyscanner and other sites track your IP address and put prices up and down based on what they determine your desire to buy. e.g if you've booked one-way and are looking for the return these sites will jack the prices up by in most cases 50%. Incognito browsing pays.

Use a VPN such as Hola to book your flight from your destination

Install Hola, change your destination, the location from which a ticket is booked can affect the price. Try using a different address when booking to take advantage of this.

Choose the right time to buy your ticket.

Choose the right time to buy your ticket, as purchasing tickets on a Sunday has been proven to be cheaper. If you can only book during the week, try to do it on a Tuesday.

Fly late for cheaper prices.

Fly late for cheaper prices. Red-eye flights, the ones that leave last in the day, are typically cheaper and less crowded, so aim to book that flight if possible. You will also get through the airport much quicker at the end of the day.

PRO TIP: Get an empty water bottle with you. Once you pass the security check, fill it with water. It will save you $5

Use this APP for same day flights

The Get the Flight Out app (iOS only) from fare tracker Hopper is a go-to choice for travelers looking for same-day flights. The inventory is from major airlines as well as low-cost carriers, and the prices are always favorable. A recent search found a British Airways round-trip from JFK Airport to London's Heathrow for $300.

Take a waterproof bag

If you're travelling alone you can swim without worrying about your phone, wallet and passport laying on the beach.

You can also use it as a source of entertainment on those ultra budget flights

Make a private entertainment centre anywhere

Always take an eye-mask, earplugs, a scarf and a kindle reader - so you can sleep and entertain yourself anywhere!

Take a sponge with you – freeze sponges to keep your food treats fresh.

As long as they are completely frozen, you won't have any problems getting them through airport security.

Travel Gadgets

The door alarm

If you're nervous and staying in private rooms or airbnbs take a door alarm. For those times when you just don't feel safe. 'When you're in a new place, an added measure of protection can give you peace of mind to sleep.

Smart Blanket

I used it when flying to Zurich. The plane was freezing, and there were no blankets to be had. I was the only one that was warm and cozy for the whole 8 hours. Amazon http://amzn.to/2hTYlOP I paid $49.00

The coat that becomes a tent

https://www.adiff.com/products/tent-jacket

Clever Tank Top with Secret Pockets

Keep your valuables safe in this top. Perfect for all climates. https://www.amazon.com/Clever-Travel-Companion-Unisex-secret/dp/B00O94PXLE

Buy on Amazon for $39.90

Convenient Water Bottle with Built-in Pill Organizer

Great way to take your medication while on the go. The medication holder can also be detached. Holding 23 oz. or 600ml, the bottle cap also doubles as a cup. Ingenious!

Optical Camera Lens for Smartphones and Tablets

Leave your bulky camera at home. Turn your device into a high-performance camera. Buy on Amazon for $9.95

Travel-sized Wireless Router with USB Media Storage

Convert any wired network to a wireless network. Buy on Amazon for $17.99

Buy a Scrubba Bag to wash your clothes on the go

Or a cheaper imitable. You can wash your clothes on the go.

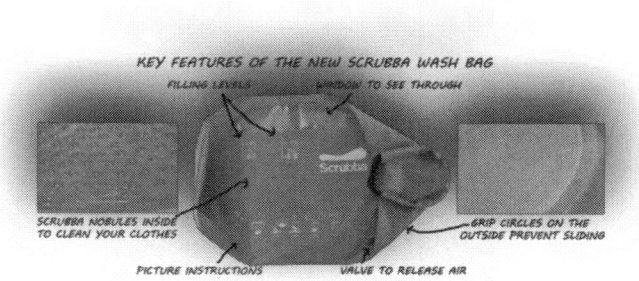

On The Road

Follow locals

Follow the locals. If there are locals around you, you're doing it right. If there are only tourists, you're probably being
ripped off.

Set-up a New Uber/ other car hailing app account for discounts

Google offers $50 free for new users in most cities when
you have a new gmail.com email account.

Couchsurfing

Totally safe when the person has reviews, but competitive.
Book early and confirm before you go. Take a tent, you'll
have somewhere to stay if the host cancels last minute.

Hitch-hiking

A good option to save money on transport which will take
up a much larger chunk of your budget but only do in
groups and let someone know when you are at all times.
Family locator app is a good way to do this automatically.

Internet

Check Foursquare for free Wi-Fi hotspots
Get a local cheap sim for data on the go.
Rewards lounges usually have unprotected Wi-Fi networks.
Buying Internet access from your mobile device rather than
your laptop can get you a better rate. Alternatively, you can
spoof your browser's User Agent.

Include external portable power battery for phone charging

Look for people already eating and drinking

Check the Spotted by Locals apps or blogs (Europe & North America)
Get the local experiences: Trip: The Happiest Way to Enjoy Truly Local Experiences (Trip is now available in 86 countries)

Checking Bags

Everyone says this, but it's always worth saying again: Never, ever check a bag if you possibly can avoid it. You're better off doing laundry a couple times in a hostel bathroom. You might also meet interesting people at a coin-op laundry.

Make sure to take a photo of your bag before you check it. This will speed up the paperwork if it is damaged or lost.

Take advantage of other hotel's amenities

Take advantage of other hotel's amenities, for example, if you fancy a swim but you're nowhere near the ocean, try the nearest hotel with a pool. As long as you buy a drink, the hotel staff will likely grant you access.

Fill up your mini bar for free.

Fill up your mini bar for free by storing things from the breakfast bar in your mini bar to give you a greater selection of drinks and food.

Save yourself some ironing

Save yourself some ironing by using the steam from the shower to get rid of wrinkles in clothing. If something is creased, leave it trapped with the steam in the bathroom overnight for even better results.

Recover from a big night out.

Recover from a big night out by using a pants hanger to secure the curtains, keeping your room nice and dark.

See somewhere else for free!

See somewhere else for free! Check to see if your flight offers free stopovers, allowing you to experience another city without spending any extra money.

Wear your heaviest clothes

on the plane to save weight in your suitcase, allowing you to bring more with you. Big coats can then be used as pillows to make your flight more comfortable.

Rebook for a cheaper change of flight.

Some airlines charge high changing fees, whereas last minute flights can be extremely cheap.

Google Your Flight Number before you leave for the airport

Easily find out where your plane is from anywhere. Confirm the status of your flight before you leave.

Protect your belongings during the flight.

Put a 'Fragile' on anything you check to ensure that it's handled better as it goes through security. It'll also be one of the first bags released after the flight, getting you out of the airport quicker.

Don't get lost while you're away.

Find where you want to go using Google Maps, then type 'OK Maps' into the search bar to store this information for offline viewing.

Dine Early

Walk-ins are often accommodated late in the afternoon, and reservations at buzzy restaurants are more plentiful then, too and lunch deals can be half the price of dinner.

Use car renting services

Drive Now or Car2Go.

Share Rides

Use sites like blablacar.com to find others who are driving in your direction. It can be 80% cheaper than normal transport. Just check the drivers reviews.

Use free gym passes

Get a free gym day pass by googling the name of a local gym and free day pass.

When asked by people providing you a service where you are from

If there's no price list for the service you are asking for, when asked where you are from, Say you are from a well-known poorer country. I normally say Macedonia, and if they don't know where it is, add it's a poor country. If you say UK, USA, the majority of Europe bar the well-known poorer countries taxi drivers, tour operators etc will match the price to what they think you pay at home

Hacks for Families

Rent an Airbnb apartment so you can cook

Apartments are much better for families, as you have all the amenities you'd have at home. They are normally cheaper per person too.

Shop at local markets

Eat seasonal products and local products. Get closer to the local market and observe the prices and the offer. What you can find more easily, will be the cheapest

Take Free Tours

Download free podcast tours of the destination you are visiting. The podcast will tell you where to start, where to go, and what to look for. Often you can find multiple podcast tours of the same place. Listen to all of them if you like, each one will tell you a little something new.

Pack Extra Ear Phones

If you go on a museum tour, they often have audio guides. Instead of having to rent one for each person, take some extra earphones. Most audio tour devices have a place to plug in a second set.

Free Hotel Breakfast

Only stay at hotels that include a free breakfast with their standard rate. If you are on a week-long family trip, this could save you a ton of money.

Buy Souvenirs Ahead of Time

If you are buying souvenirs someone touristy, you are paying a premium price. By ordering the same exact products online, you can save a lot of money.

Use Cheap Transportation

Do as the locals do, including weekly passes.

Carry a Reusable Water Bottle

Spending money on water and other beverages can quickly add up. Instead of paying for drinks, take some refillable water bottles.

Combine Attractions

Many major cities offer ticket bundles where one price gets you into 5 or 6 popular attractions. You will need to plan ahead of time to decide what things you plan to do on vacation and see if they are selling these activities together.

Pack Snacks

Granola bars, apples, baby carrots, bananas, cheese crackers, juice boxes, pretzels, fruit snacks, apple sauce, grapes, and veggie chips.

Stick to Carry-On Bags

Do not pay to check a large bag. Even a small child can pull a carry-on.

Visit free art galleries and museums

Just google the name + free days.

Eat Street Food

There's a lot of unnecessary fear around this. You can watch the food prepared. Go for the stands that have a steady queue.

Travel Gadgets for Families

Dropcam

Are what-if scenarios playing out in your head? Then you need Dropcam.

'Dropcam HD Internet Wi-Fi Video Monitoring Cameras help you watch what you love from anywhere. In less than a minute, you'll have it setup and securely streaming video to you over your home Wi-Fi. Watch what you love while away with Dropcam HD.'

Approximate Price: $139

Kelty-Child-Carrier

Voted as one of the best hiking essentials if you're traveling with kids and can carry a child up to 18kg.

Jetkids Bedbox

No more giving up your own personal space on the plane.

How to earn money WHILE travelling

1. Online english teaching job $20 - you will need a private room for this. - https://t.vipkid.com.cn/?refereeId=3262664
2. Work in a hostel. Normally you'll get some cash and free accommodation.
3. Fruit picking. I picked Bananas in Tully Australia for $20 an hour. The jobs are menial but can be quite meditative.
4. You could work on luxury yachts in the med. Its hard work, but you can save money - DesperateSailors.com
5. fiverr.com - offer a small service, like making a video template and changing the content for each buyer.
6. upwork.com - you need to put in a lot of work to make this successful, but if you have a unique skill like coding, or marketing it can be lucrative.
7. Make a udemy.com course
8. Use skype to deliver all manner of services, language lessons, therapy etc. Google for what you could offer. Most speclaisoms have a platform you can use to find clients and they will take a cut of your earnings/ require a fee.
9. Become an Airbnb experience host - but this requires you to know one place and stay there for a time. And you will need a work visa for that country.
10. WWOOF.org which focuses on organic farm work.
11. Rent your place out on airbnb while you travel and get a cleaner to manage it.

Safety

I always check fco.co.uk before travelling. NEVER RELY on websites or books. Things are changing constantly and the FCO's advice is always UP TO DATE and extremely conservative.

I've travelled alone to over 150 countries and the main thing I learnt is if you walk around scared, or anticipating you're going to be pickpocketed, your constant fear will attract bad energy. Murders or attacks on travellers are the mainstay of media, not reality, especially in countries familiar with travellers. The only place I had cause to genuinely fear for my life was Papa New Guinea - where nothing actually happened to me only my own panic over culture shock.

There are many things you can do to stop yourself being victim to the two main problems when travelling: theft or being scammed.

I will address theft first. Here are my top tips. Take these with a pinch of salt, I've written them whilst in India, which can be sketchy if you're travelling alone.

- Stay alert while you're out and always have an exit strategy (no alleyways when alone).
- Keep your money in a few different places on your person and your passport somewhere it can't be grabbed.
- Take a photo of your passport on your phone incase (I never lost of had mine stolen in 15 years of constant travel). If you do lose it, google for your embassy, you can usually get a temporary pretty fast.
- Google safety tips for traveling in your country to help yourself out and memorise the emergency number.
- At hostels keep your large bag in the room far under the bed/out of the way with a lock on the zipper.

- I keep all money, valuables, passport, etc on me in my day bag. And at night I keep larger bag locked and my day bag in bed next to me/under my pillow depending on how secure the rest of the facilities are. I will alter any of the above based on circumstance or comfortability, for example, the presence of lockers or how many people in the room.
- On buses/trains I would definitely have a lock on the zippers of all bags and I would even lock it to the luggage rack if you want to sleep/if this is a notoriously sketchy route. Bag theft on Indian trains for example is very common.
- I hate constantly checking my bags and having anxiety over it. I bring a small lock for all zippers (with important things not in easily accessible pockets.
- Get a personal keychain alarm. The sound will scare anyone away.
- Don't wear any jewellery. A man attempted to rob a friend of her engagement ring in Bogota, Colombia, and in hindsight I wished I'd told her to leave it at home/wear it on a hidden necklace, as the chaos it created was avoidable.
- Don't hold your phone out while in the street.
- Don't turn your back to traffic while you use your phone.
- When traveling in the tuktuk sit in the middle and keep your bag secure. Wear sunglasses as dust can easily get in your eyes.
- Watch your bag - make sure your zippers are closed and you're aware of your things.
- Don't let anyone give you flowers, bracelets, or any type of trinket, even if they insist it's for free and compliment you like crazy.
- Be careful at night & while drinking.
- Don't go solo on excursions that take you away from crowds.
- Let someone know where you are if you are fearful. Use the family app.
- Don't let strangers know that you are alone - unless they are travel friends ;-) in fact, this is more for avoiding scams or men if you are a women travelling alone.
- Lastly, and most importantly -Trust your gut! If it doesn't feel right, it isn't.

Our Writers

Phil Tang has traveled a number of places using Lonely Planet guides and finds them to be incredibly useful; however, their recommendations for restaurants and accommodation are WAY OUT of my budget. Plus any estimation of cost was always widely inaccurate. So over the past 14 years I started compiling the Super Cheap Guides guides for people like me, who want a guide within a set budget, but one that doesn't compromise on fun.

Ali Blythe has been writing about amazing places for 17 years. He loves travel and especially tiny budgets equalling big adventures nearly as much as his family. He recently trekked the Satopanth Glacier trekking through those ways from where no one else would trek. A adventure by nature and bargainist by religion, his written over 200 guides for people travelling on a budget.

Michele Whitter writes about languages and travel. What separates her from other travel writers is her will to explain complex topics in a no-nonsense, straightforward manner. She doesn't promise the world. But always delivers step-by-step strategies you can immediately implement to travel on a small Budget.

Kim Mortmier whether it's a two-week, two-month, or two-year trip, Kim's input on Super Cheap Guides Travel Guides show you how to stretch your money further so you can travel cheaper, smarter, and with more wanderlust. She loves going over land on horses.

Copyright

Published in Great Britain in 2018 by Bloom House Press LTD.

Copyright © 2018 Bloom House Press LTD.

The right of Phil G A Tang to be identified as the Author of the Work has been asserted in accordance with the Copyright, Designs and Patents Act 1988.

All rights reserved.

No part of this publication may be reproduced, stored in a retrieval system, or transmitted, in any form or by any means without the prior written permission of the publisher, nor be otherwise circulated in any form of binding or cover other than that in which it is published and without a similar condition being imposed on the subsequent purchaser.

All rights reserved. No part of this publication may be reproduced, distributed, or transmitted in any form or by any means, including photocopying, recording, or other electronic or mechanical methods, without the prior written permission of the publisher, except in the case of brief quotations embodied in critical reviews and certain other non-commercial uses permitted by copyright law.

WHAT CAN WE DO BETTER?

Tell us your wishes and we'll incorporate them. We update each guide monthly.

Traveladdictguides.com

TINY BUDGET GUIDES

WHERE NEXT?

TWO WEEKS
IN PERU FOR
$250

TWO WEEKS
IN BOLIVIA
FOR $250

7 DAYS IN
ENGLAND FOR
$250

BIG EXPERIENCES FOR TINY BUDGETS.

61905977R00067

Made in the USA
Columbia, SC
27 June 2019